The quatrains of Abu'l-Ala;

Ahmad ibn 'Abd Allah, Abu al-'Ala, al-Ma'arri, 973-1058

THE QUATRAINS OF
ABU'L-ALA

TITLE PAGE OF AN ARABIC MS. OF ABU'L-ALA'S
WRITINGS WITH THE STAMP OF THE
KHEDIVIAL LIBRARY

(Reproduced by permission of the Director of the Khedivial Library at
Cairo, Egypt)

The Quatrains
of
Abu'l-Ala

Selected from his
" Lozum-ma-la-Yalzam " and " Sact-Uz-Zind "
and now first rendered into English

By
AMEEN F. RIHANI

LONDON
Grant Richards
1904

PREFACE

WHEN all Europe was arming itself for the first crusade, when the Northmen were ravaging the western world with their marauding expeditions, when the Califs were engaged in bloody battle with their rebellious subjects, Abu'l-Ala was waging his silent and bloodless war on the follies and evils of his age. He attacked the superstitions and the false traditions of religions, and proclaimed the supremacy of the mind; he hurled his trenchant invectives at the tyranny and despotism of rulers, and asserted the supremacy of the human soul; he stood for perfect equality, and fought against the fallacies, the shams and the lies of the ruling class of his time, in its social, religious and political aspects.

This man lived in the latter part of the tenth and the first half of the eleventh centuries, and the European world of knowledge has succeeded in ignoring him for the nine centuries that followed. Nothing is so remarkable as the slight mention of him, even by Arabic writers and historians.

Abu'l-Ala'l-Märri, the Lucretius of Al-Islam, the Diogenes of Arabia and the Voltaire of the East, first saw the light in the spring of the year 974 A. D., in the small and obscure village of Marrah, near Aleppo. His real name is Ahmed ibn Abdallah ibn Soleiman, etc., and his surname, Abu'l-Ala, signifying "the father of the sublime," is the fitting appellation which his contemporary admirers have spontaneously conferred upon him. His real name is only known to biography and history, while throughout the Arabic-speaking world he is popularly known as Abu'l-Ala.

When a boy, his father taught him the first principles of grammar, and thus instilled in his mind a love for learning. Subsequently he was sent to Aleppo, where, with a private tutor, he pursued his studies. His poetical tendencies were developed in his boyhood, and his first attempts were made when only eleven years of age. These early compositions were not, however, preserved.

Preface

When he fell a victim to smallpox and almost
lost his sight by reason thereof, he had barely
completed his fifth year. A weakness in his
eyes continued thereafter to trouble him, and
he became, in middle age, I presume, totally
blind. Some of his biographers would have
us believe that he was born blind; others say
that he completely lost his sight when he was
attacked by the virulent disease; and still others
intimate that he could see slightly at least with
one eye. As to whether or not he was blind
when he went to Aleppo to pursue his studies
his biographers do not say. My theory, based
on the careful perusal of his poems and on a
statement advanced by one of his biographers,*
is that he lost his sight gradually, and only
became totally blind either in his youth or his

---

*"He was four years of age when attacked with small-
pox. His right eyeball turned white and his left eye was
entirely lost Says Al-Hafez As-Salafi: 'Abu Mohammed
Abdallah tells me that he visited him (Abu'l-Ala) once,
with his uncle, and found him sitting on an old hair
matting. He was very old, and the disease that
attacked him in his boyhood had left its deep traces on
his emaciated face. He asked me to come near him, and
blessed me as he placed his hand on my head. I was a
boy then, and I can picture him before me now. I look
into his eyes, and remember well how the one was horribly
protruding and the other completely buried in its socket
and could not be seen.'"— Ibn-Khollakan's "Lives of
Eminent Men."

middle age. Were we to believe that he was born blind, or that he completely lost his sight in his boyhood, we should be at a loss to know, not how he wrote his poems, for he always dictated to about ten amanuenses; not how he taught his pupils, for that was done by lectures; but how he was taught and instructed himself, in the absence of a regular system of instruction for the blind at that time.

He visited Bagdad, the centre of learning and intelligence and the capital of the Abbaside Califs, in his twenty-fifth year, and remained there about nineteen months, during which period he became acquainted with most of the learned men of his time. He attended the lectures of the leading Sufis and doctors, and listened with care and attention to their subtle arguments and fustian declamations on religion, philosophy and science.

It is also said in "Al-Muktataf," volume 10, page 450, that he journeyed to Tripoli and added much to his store of knowledge from its public library; and that, stopping on his way back at Lazekeiiah, he lodged in a monastery and there met a monk learned in theology and metaphysics, who discoursed with him on these subjects. From that time he began to doubt and to question.

There are virtually the only data extant showing the various sources of Abu'l-Ala's knowledge. His keen perception, his powerful intellect, his prodigious memory, together with a feverish desire to learn, render these means and sources sufficient for him, though scanty for others with less aptitude and aspiration. He was especially noted for the extraordinary memory he possessed; and around this fact biographers and historians weave a thick net of stories, which must be relegated to the dark world of myths. I have no doubt that one with such a prodigious memory could retain in a few minutes what the average person cannot; but when we are told that Abu'l-Ala once heard one of his pupils speaking with a friend in a foreign language, and repeated, then and there, the long conversation, word for word, without having the faintest idea of its meaning, we are disposed to be skeptical. Many like stories are recorded and repeated by historians and biographers, without as much as intimating a doubt in their authenticity. I take it for granted that he possessed a prodigious memory, but the fact that he was blind answers partly, I think, for its abnormal development.

His career as poet and scholar actually dates from the time he returned from Bagdad. This, as far as I know, was the last journey he ever made, and his home thenceforth became his earthly prison. He calls himself "a recluse in two prisons," his solitude being the one and his blindness the other. Like most of the scholars of his age, in the absence of regular institutions of learning, with perhaps one or two exceptions, he had to devote a part of his time to the large number of pupils that flocked to Marrah from all parts of Asia Minor, Arabia and India. Rapidly his fame was growing, and his early compositions won for him the support of all the prominent princes and rulers of his time.

On every possible and known subject he dictated to his numerous amanuenses. He is not only a poet of the first rank, but an essayist, a literary critic and a mathematician as well. Everything he wrote, or, rightly speaking, dictated, was transcribed by the thousands of his votaries, as was the fashion then, and thus circulated far and near. Nothing, however, was preserved but two of his Diwans, and a volume of essays, of which I shall yet have occasion to speak.

His reputation as poet and scholar had now overlept the horizons, as one historian has it. Honours were conferred upon him successively by both the rulers and the writers of his age. His many noted admirers in the Far and the Near East were in constant communication with him. He was now considered the master of the learned, the chief of the wise, and the sole king of the bards of his century. Märrah became the Mecca of every literary aspirant; ambitious young men came there to be instructed, to be informed, to be inspired. Abu'l-Ala received them all with open arms and, though a pessimist, with a smile; he imparted to them what he knew, and told them frankly what he would not teach, since, unlike other scholars, he was not able to grasp the truth nor even compass one of the smallest mysteries of creation. In his latter days, when a venerable old man, youthful admirers came to be blessed, been stricken with blindness, and had not smallpox disfigured his features, he would have found a palliative in society. His pessimism might not have been cured, but it would have been rendered at least enticing rather than stinging. Nor is his strong aversion for marriage, in view of these facts, surprising.

He lived to know that "his fame spread from the sequestered village which he inhabited to the utmost confines of the globe"; he died in the year 1058 A. D., completing his eighty-four years of age, and was buried in a garden surrounding his home. Al-Hafez tells us that there were present around his grave more than one hundred and eighty poets, and that he was eulogized by eighty-four speakers, among whom were the foremost doctors, scholars and writers of his time. Americans and Europeans may think this a very large draft on their credulity; but when they bear in mind that almost every one who studied Arabic grammar had also to study prosody and versification, and thus become a poet, or, at least, a rhymster, the draft would not appear so large. The Arabs were born poets, and the death of a noted person among them is always an occasion for much display of exuberant and grandiloquent eulogies.

Abu'l-Ala, besides being a poet of the first rank, was also the foremost and profoundest thinker of his age, not excepting his learned contemporary, Ibn-Sina, known to European scholars as Avicenna. Very little is said of his teachings, his characteristics, and his many-sided and brilliant intellectual career in the biographies I have read. The fact that he was a liberal thinker, a trenchant writer, a free, candid and honest man, answers for this neglect on the part of Mohammedan writers, who tried to conceal from us what his poems unquestionably reveal.

The larger collection of these poems was published in 1891, in two volumes, by and under the supervision of Azeez Bey Zind, of Cairo, from an original manuscript written in the twelfth century, under Abu'l-Ala's own title, "Lozum-ma-la-Yalzam," or "The Necessity of What Is Unnecessary." This title refers to the special method of rhyming which the poet adopted. These poems, consisting of didactic

Preface

odes and quatrains, published in desultory fashion, were written, it seems, at different periods of his life, and are arranged according to the alphabetical system of rhyming, which he has chosen to adopt. They bear no headings except, "And He Also Says, Rhyming With So and So," whatever the rhyming may be. These odes and quatrains follow strictly each other, not in sequence of thought, but, as I said, in the alphabetical order of their rhyme-ending. The other small volume of heroic and miscellaneous odes is also published in Cairo by Ameen Hindiyeh. These three volumes constitute all that is now extant of his poems.

In his preface to "Lozum-ma-la-Yalzam," he says:

"It happened that during the past years I have composed these poems, and in them I have abided strictly to the true and the real. They are certainly free from lies and exaggerations. Some of them are written in glorification of God, who is, I know, above all such glory, and others are, as it were, a reminder to those who forget, a pinch to those who sleep, and a warn-

xvi

ing to those who fall in love with a world in which man is deprived of his rights and Nature deprived of the gratitude of man."

As for the translation of these chosen quatrains, let me say, at the outset, that it is almost impossible to adhere to the letter and convey the meaning without being insipid, dull, and even ridiculous at times. There being no affinity between the Arabic and the English languages, their standards of art and beauty widely differ, and in the process of transformation the outer garment at times must necessarily be doffed. I have always, however, adhered to the spirit and preserved the native imagery where it was not too clannish and grotesque. I have added nothing that was foreign to the ruling idea, nor have I omitted anything that was necessary to the completion of the general thought.

As I said before, our philosopher-poet was completely ignored by Oriental scholars, and, as far as I know, none of his poems, with only one exception, are translated to either French, German or English. J. D. Carlisle, in his "Specimen of Arabic Poetry," published in

Preface

1810, has given us a paraphrastic translation
of one of Abu'l-Ala's quatrains on " Pride and
Virtue." He also translated into Latin one of
his bold epigrams, fearing, I suppose, to pub-
lish it in English at that time.

The quatrains that are published here are
culled from the three volumes of his poems;
and they are arranged, as far as possible, in the
logical order of their sequence of thought.
They form a kind of eclogue which the poet and
scholar delivers from his prison, in Märrah.

And before closing these remarks, I must here
record my appreciation of the assistance rendered me by Lee Fairchild in the final prepara-
tion of this translation; lastly, I wish to call
attention to a question which, though unim-
portant in itself, is nevertheless worthy of the
consideration of every admirer of Arabic and
Persian literature. I refer to the similarity
of thought that exists between Omar Khayyam
and Abu'l-Ala. The former, I have reason to
believe, was an imitator or a disciple of the
latter. The birth of the first and the death of
the second poets are not very far apart from
each other; they both occurred about the middle

of the eleventh century. The English-reading public, here and abroad, has already formed its opinion of Khayyam, and let it not, therefore, be supposed that in making this claim I aim to shake or undermine its great faith. Nor am I so presumptuous as to think that one could succeed in such a hazardous undertaking. My desire is to confirm and not to convulse, to expand and not to contract the Oriental influence on Occidental minds.

Whoever will take the trouble, however, to read Omar Khayyam in conjunction with what is here translated of Abu'l-Ala, cannot fail, if he discern rightly, to see that the skepticism and pessimism of Omar are, to a great extent, imported from Márrah. In his religious opinions the Arabian philosopher is far more outspoken than the Persian poet. I do not say that Omar was a plagiarist, but I say this: Just as Voltaire, for instance, acquired most of his liberal and skeptical views from Hobbes, Locke and Bayle, so did Omar acquire his from Abu'l-Ala. In my notes to these quatrains I have quoted, in comparison, from both the Fitzgerald and the Heron-Allen versions of the

Persian poet, and with so much or so little said,
I leave the matter in charge of the reader, who,
on a careful examination, will doubtless bear
me out on this point.

AMEEN F. RIHANI.

THE QUATRAINS OF ABU'L-ALA

I

BEHOLD the Night, lest vauntingly we say,
    "He fell a-bleeding, 'neath the sword
        of Day,"
Again recharges with his starry host,
While all the fiery Suns in ambush lay.

II

O, Night, to me thou art as bright, as fair
As Dawn or Twilight, with their golden hair;
    How oft, when young, we lurked beneath
        thy wing,
And Jupiter, with bated breath, would stare!

III

Our eyes, all heedless of sweet Sleep's behest:
Scanned in God's book of Stars the sonnet best,
    The Pleiads—ah, the Moon from them
        departs;
She throws a kiss and hastens toward the west.

IV

But soon my Night, this winsome Ethiop Queen,
Who passes by be-jewelled, calm, serene,
    Will wax old and with Saffron deeply dye
Her tresses, lest the ash of age be seen.

V

Our Nights and Days around each other spin,
And we like Planets end as we begin;
    Our feet are on the heads of those that
        passed,
And as the Cradle cries, the Graves all grin.

VI

This Life-span will between two Shores e'er
swing;
We cross it, and who knows what's on the wing?
I never could, tho' long upon the bridge,
Like billows moan, ah me, nor wind-like sing.

VII

Our Joys and Griefs, each other oft revile;
They come and go, enduring but awhile;
  The Clouds, that shed their tears on land
    and sea,
Have Lightning-lips, whose laugh the tears
    beguile.

VIII

What boots it, in my creed, that Man should
    moan
In Sorrow's Night, or sing in Pleasure's Dawn?
    In vain the doves all coo on yonder branch—
In vain one sings or sobs: behold ! he's gone.

IX

So solemnly the Funeral passes by!
The march of Triumph, under this same sky,
    Comes in its trail—both vanish into Night:
To me are one, the Sob, the Joyous Cry.

X

Behold, O, friend, our tombs engulf the land,

Our fathers' corses moulder in the sand;

  From Aad's time where and how many

    are the graves?

Has not this sea of Death a cliff, a strand?

XI

Thus they have passed, and we shall follow soon
Into an endless Midnight or a Noon;
    The Stars, that likewise oft shoot from
        their spheres,
Fall in the arms of wooing Sun or Moon.

XII

Tread lightly, for a thousand hearts unseen
Might now be beating in this misty green;
    Here are the herbs that once were pretty
        cheeks,
Here the remains of those that once have been.

XIII

Many a Grave embraces friend and foe,
And grins in scorn at this most sorry show;
    A multitude of corses therein pressed—
Alas! Time almost reaps e'er he doth sow!

XIV

The warp and woof of Life are woe and gloom;
The Cup is bitter; endless pain the doom:
    Strange then that he should weave, that
        he should drink,
Who knows well how to smash both Cup and
        Loom!

XV

The Days devour us all; none will they spare,

And fang'd hours, Lion-like, upon us stare;

    Anon they bound, and twixt their teeth

        we groan,

Anon return to their eternal Lair!

XVI

We're only moved from this all battered Tent
To some abode of peace, by accident;
    A night of deep sleep and repose is Death,
While in Life's day this Sleep by Care is rent.

XVII

Every abode to Ruin is addrest,

Be it a palace or a sparrow's nest;

   Let not the mighty build, for they must go,

Like that fair dove, with what they built, to rest.

XVIII

Why drinkest from the fountain of Belief?
Why seekest at the Saki's door relief?
    A lie imbibed, a thousand lies will breed,
And in the end thyself will come to grief.

XIX

A-fearing whom I trust I gain my end,

But trusting, without fear, I lose, my friend;

    Much better is the Doubt that gives me

        peace,

Than all the Faiths which in hell-fire may end.

XX

Upon Hypocrisy and Cant we speed,

Our hobbies all are of a sickly breed;

  Doubt then in all things, doubt the very

    age,

Doubt that he is good who does a good deed.

XXI

Ye weeping daughters of Hadeel, I pray,

A word of comfort to a Doubter say;

    Would I were thee, and thou wert me to

        fool

This restless, aye, and dream-like life away.

XXII

I sometimes think myself here to complete
A problem sad, with X's all replete;
    Despite myself I bridled am by Fate,
And at the bottom, ah, there's nothing meet.

XXIII

How oft around the Well my Soul would grope
Athirst; but lo! my Pail was without Rope:
    I cried for Water, and the deep, dark Well
Echoed my wailing cry, but not my hope.

XXIV

The I, in me, combats oft with this Soul,

Who scorns the Pail, and fain would seek the
Whole;

But how to rise once fallen in the Depth,

And how protect the Branches from the Bole?

XXV

"How long," she says, "will I this burden bear—
How long this tattered garment will I wear?"
    Why doff it not, why throw not down the
      load,
And thus unburdened the Hyperion dare?

XXVI

If Consciousness in after-life prevail,
I will the Secrets all with it unveil;
    But if, like flesh, alas! it melt away,
My sighs and yearnings all will not avail.

XXVII

The door of Certainty we can't unlock,
But we can knock and guess and guess and
       knock:
  Night quickly carries us upon its Sail,
Ship-like, but where, O Night-ship, is thy dock?

XXVIII

O Death's Typhoon, in thy e'er whirling storm,
Thou sparest neither man, nor beast, nor worm;
    Behind thy hell, is there a Will divine,
That would remould us into better form?

XXIX

How like so many coins in Fate's big hand
We are, and Fate will always lavish and
    Alas! the good Coin is so quickly spent,
While all the bad Coins linger in the land.

XXX

Ye sons of men, pray take it not to heart
If I do thee arraign, as all or part;
    Since freely with myself I will begin,
And lo! my truth is bold and void of art.

XXXI

Among us some are great and some are small,
Albeit in wickedness, we're masters all;
    Or, if my fellow men are like myself,
The human race shall always rise and fall.

XXXII

The air of sin I breathe without restraint;

With selfishness my few good deeds I taint;

I come as I was moulded and I go,

But near the vacant shrine of Truth I faint.

XXXIII

I laugh and lo ! my shafts of scorn doth leap
On Adam's sons, who all by right should weep;
    Doubt crushes us like glass, and even the
        hope
Of restoration lost is in the heap.

XXXIV

Like all of us, I, too, do lie and cheat,

And hope to mend, before my death I meet;

    But Time cries out,"Make haste and purge

        thy soul,

To-morrow's dawn thou mayst not live to greet."

XXXV

Life's mystic curtain, held by Destiny,
Its darkest shadow now casts over me;
    It rises—and behold, I act my part;
It falls—and who knows what and where I'll be?

XXXVI

My Soul, I often most sincerely warn,
But all my warnings she receives with scorn;
   My sins are sands upon the shore of Life,
Alack! the Day when Death will blow his horn!

XXXVII

O friend, those foul and sorry deeds of mine,
This soul, tho' deep and broad, incarnadine;
    If they were written on the face of Dawn,
The Sun himself would stop, recede and pine.

XXXVIII

But from necessity, without intent
I sin; wherefore a future punishment?
    "The harmless piece of steel becomes a
        sword,
With God's foreknowledge," say they, "and
        consent."

XXXIX

How oft, when young, my friends I would
defame,
If our religious faiths were not the same;
But now my Soul has travelled high and
low—
Now all save Love, to me, is but a name:

XL

A church, a temple, or a Kaba Stone,
Koran or Bible or a martyr's bone—
    All these and more my heart can tolerate
Since my religion now is Love alone.

XLI

To all humanity, O consecrate
Thy heart, and shun the thousand Sects that
      prate
    About the things they little know about—
Let all receive thy pity, love, or hate.

XLII

The sheik who, in his mosque the bigot cows,
Is much like unto him who doth carouse:
    The one is drunk with pride and mad
        conceit,
The other bravely breaks his foolish vows.

XLIII

"The grape juice is forbidden," say these folk,
But they the law will for themselves revoke;
   The sheik tells thee he is without a garb,
When in the tap-house he has pawned his cloak.

XLIV

Their mosques and brothels are to me the same,
Their prayers are blasphemies on Allah's name;
    If pulpits will revolt not, when the sheiks
Pose in them as our teachers, who's to blame?

XLV

Every Friday, from these pulpits spring
A thousand lies, to calm a monstrous king;
    They ask that God preserve his life, and he
Carouses while young damsels round him sing.

XLVI

But Destiny, my friends, will always plot;
Change then is constant—wealth and power not;
    And he who drinks to-day in a golden bowl
May drink to-morrow in a wooden pot.

XLVII

If prayers produce among us this rich crop
Of vice, abandon prayers and wed the cup;
    Drink, whilst thou art of this Mortality,
When dead thou mayst not ever taste a drop.

XLVIII

Awake, awake, thou pious dupes, awake!
And see how all the creeds and cults do shake:
    These are the jades the wily ancients rode
Upon the track of Life, to win their stake.

XLIX

Their sons cry out and clamour, vaunt and
      swell,
Seeking the ocean, with their shrieks to quell;
    The thunder hath some charm, but does
      not rain
Without quench the thirst of earth as well?

L

Their vices 'neath the veil of Faith they hide,
And thus parade them, with unbridled pride;
 Our reason we abuse, when we believe
Their Lies, and Reason is the only guide.

LI

"What is thy faith?" these creeping cuckolds
        cry;
Others into my pedigree would pry:
    I'm one of Allah's sons, the world my tent,
The human race my tribe, until I die.

LII

The voiceless, countless Army of our Time
Invades the darkest and the brightest clime—
   The human soul, under its burning feet
Still groans, and Time, alas! is in his prime.

LIII

Howbeit these sages say, "The end is here,"
That death will take the worlds, afar and near;
    They lie about the universe, and—well,
Heed not their threats, and yield thou not to
    fear.

LIV

These good astrologers are blind, indeed;
The page of Fate, by touch, they try to read;
    In vain they strive the letters to construct,
Which only in confusing they succeed.

LV

Another prophet will, they say, soon rise;
But will he profit by his tricks, likewise?
　　My prophet is my reason, aye, myself—
From me to me there is no room for lies.

LVI

How many preachers from the pulpits preach,

How many prophets rose from sleep to teach?

    They prayed, and slayed, and passed away,

        and yet

Our ills are like the pebbles on the beach!

LVII

These Superstitions, Sacred Books and Creeds,
These Cults and Myths and other noxious
Weeds—
So many Lies are crowned, in every age,
While Truth beneath the tyrant's heel still
bleeds.

LVIII

Aye, Wrong forever is proclaimed aloud,
And strongly yoked upon a boundless crowd;
    But Truth is only whispered to the few,
Who bury it alive without a shroud.

LIX

When all are silent, thou wilt have to say,
But silent be thyself the while they bray;
    Sound Wisdom warns thee—"if thou wilt
        be right,
Then differ from them all, and go thy way."

LX

Seek not their guidance! Hush, and walk
    alone,
Among us Reason can not hold her own;
    The Pearl that comes to human hands
      will break,
But in the Deep 'tis safe upon her throne.

LXI

What! shun the Sun that guides thy battered
     Bark,
And seek the flash of Lightning in the Dark?
    Cannot thy sins withstand his searching
     light?
Can not thy Soul on Heaven's wing embark?

LXII

Throughout the East and West reign fell
            discords
About the Creeds, among the Chiefs and Lords;
    If Creeds, however, differ in their text,
They all concur in being spurious frauds!

LXIII

The Time is Allah's, and this noise and din
About the Sabbaths all is worse than sin;
  What profits it, what glory can there be,
If Friday should retreat and Sunday win?

LXIV

Throughout the Ages we have cringed and crept
And 'neath the feet of Masters few have slept;
    O, have they, friend, to lift us ever stoopt—
Have they with Rabbik promise ever kept?

LXV

Oppression waits, and waiting he prepares
For vengeance 'gainst his former Lords and
heirs;
He serves their tyranny awhile and lo!
He drags them soon or late into their snares!

LXVI

The Laws among us fell discord create;
They teach us how to plot, and steal, and hate;
    Why worship then their makers? why
        obey
The Judges who on Mammon ever wait?

LXVII

I'm weary of my stay in this broad land,

Where princes rob and slay by God's command;

    Long have they ruled us, we the Masters

      true,

When shall we, O, when shall we wield the wand?

LXVIII

Virtue and Pride cannot each other greet;
As Youth and Age themselves can never meet;
    When this one grows the other shrinks,
        and when
The Night is long the Day is not complete.

LXIX

If thou to wealth and power be allied,
Fang'd Cares upon thy soul will naked ride;
    But be thou languid, poor and ignorant,
And Happiness will be thy loving bride.

LXX

Or wed thyself to Reason and behold
The Snakes of persecution (young and old,
    Around thee hissing, poisoning the well
Of Life's Devotion true) their net unfold.

LXXI

O, pitch my tent upon the desert sand,

Far from the fawner and the carper's land.

    Some think me pious, rich and learned, too,

But they between all these and me e'er stand.

LXXII

My ignorance of things I do confess,

My Nothingness to Something I address;

  Howbeit, there are those who think
    wise,

And those who—ah, but even these I bless

LXXIII

If there be one who in this world succeeds,
I bear with him, to brag about his deeds;
    But when he feigns to be my loving friend,
I break upon his back an hundred reeds!

LXXIV

My months, as dull and vapid as my lay,
Are repetitions of one gloomy day;
   My heart has learned to scoff at them, and
      now
December fear I not, nor fondle May.

LXXV

The ways and means of Destiny I've known—
In me her sorry Scheme is deeply sown;
    All her misfortunes I receive in cash,
But Joy she pays in drafts on Heaven drawn.

LXXVI

So oft the Fates with ill-luck did assail

This Soul, that now they strike without avail—

    A thousand spears all shield my bleeding

        heart,

And steel now breaks on steel—the blow will

        fail.

LXXVII

This Life is in itself a foul disease,

Which Galen could not cure, nor Bocrates;

    These were themselves in its unyielding

        grip,

And only Death would hear their fervent pleas.

LXXVIII

A Soul that had not entered yet a pot
Longed, from her height, to throw with ours
      her lot;
  She sent a harbinger to sound the Depth;
The harbinger below cried out: "Do not!"

LXXIX

O, when will Fate come forth with his decree,
That I may clasp the cool clay and be free?
  My Soul and Body, wedded for awhile,
Are sick and would that separation be.

LXXX

Do yonder birds, that labour with such zest,

Know, like ourselves, that there can be no rest?

    Were they but conscious of the world's
    design,

They would not build their young that cozy nest.

LXXXI

Hunt not the beast; O, be thou more humane,
Since hunter here nor hunted long remain;
    The smallest grub a life has in it which
Thou canst not take without inflicting pain.

LXXXII

The few among us are the Sparks that prance
Upon the top within the Cup of Chance;
    They quickly rise and quickly disappear,
And when you shake the Cup again they dance.

LXXXIII

Why weedest thou the garden of the Soul,
If on the Wheel of Life thou wouldst yet roll?
    'Tis true, most noxious are some plants
        therein;
But pluck them, if thou wilt impair the whole.

LXXXIV

Behold, the veil that hid thy Soul is torn,
And all thy secrets on the winds are borne;
    The hand of Sin has written on thy face—
"Awake, for these untimely furrows warn!"

LXXXV

Why wonder if the Raven pass away
To make place for the Falcon's brighter day?
    For shame !   I see the mirror in thy hand—
The tweezers, too—wilt thou defeat his play?

LXXXVI

Hast thou not read the Manuscript of Time,

All dotted by Misfortune and by Crime?

    Hast thou not pondered on it—hast thou

        not

Rejoiced and gloried in its tone sublime?

LXXXVII

Then get thee hence, for thou art like the tomb,
Which takes from us, to rot and to consume,
  The dearest that we cherish and the best,
And pays us nothing back—ah, me ! the doom.

LXXXVIII

O, shake my dust from off thy feet and doff
Thy cloak of Love, Devotion and like stuff—
 I'm but a gust of wind on desert sand—
Enough of thy duplicity, enough!

LXXXIX

Canst not thou to the thousand sullied Beads
Upon thy String add one pearl of good Deeds?
The marvels of Creation all reveal
That which I doubt not, tho' I doubt the Creeds.

XC

Heed thou my counsel, by it well abide—
A traveller gone astray will hear his guide;
   Howbeit, disciples might defeat my hope,
If freely on Illusion's wing they ride.

XCI

Thy wealth can shed no tears around thy bier,
Nor can it rob thee of thy woe or fear;
    Ere thou departest, with it freely part—
Let poor folk plead for thee and He will hear.

XCII

For me thy silks and feathers have no charm,
The pillow I like best is my right arm;
    The comforts of your Passing Show I spurn
In travelling, and I heed not your alarm.

XCIII

The blind man's staff is faithful, sound and true,
Unlike the friends and guides who round him
     drew :—
     Come, then, thou dumb and silent piece of
     oak,
No son of Eve shall walk with me and you.

XCIV

The luxuries of kings I envy not,

When a truffle and some beans fall to my lot;

    I drink rejoicing with my naked hands—

I sigh not for the Saki and his pot.

XCV

Nay, in a wry, old earthen bowl I drink,
Tho' in a sea of pearls and gold I sink;
    The wooden shoes I do like best because
That skin did once live, aye, and even think.

XCVI

Withal, my shoes and clothes do heavily weigh
On me, and Freedom has no right of way;
    I care not for them, when I think I have
To don and doff them every night and day.

XCVII

O, fie upon thee, Mother Earth! O, fie!
In all thy games we cheat, and lose and lie;
> Divorced thou would'st be if thou wert a
> wife,
But no true son his Mother will decry.

XCVIII

No, in the Khodour I have never been,
Nor e'en the Black Stone have I kissed or seen—
    Cold death alone lurks in the Serpents' den—
And the Kābas all my Soul can never clean.

XCIX

I wish to stand, like Adam, at one end
Of this long line, which I shall not extend;
    Tho' Omar yawns as Khalid does, I can
Not be infected by the Yawn, my friend.

C

This pleasure, born of pain and misery,
No wretched Soul inherit shall from me;
    I dig not, like the Lizard, for her cubs,
Nor bird-like toil and moil for chicks to be.

CI

My Goal's the grave, my Hours are my good
steed;
My Life the road on which I blindly speed;
  A little while and then the One unseen
Strikes, and behold! I'm but a sapless weed.

CII

He who the learned puzzled all the way,
The sages keeping constantly at play—
    To them a secret hidden—is to me
Only an animal evolved of Clay.

CIII

A reeling Branch would not hold high his head,
If he were laden with some fruits instead
    Of withered leaves. "But why bear fruits,"
        he says,
"If bending 'neath my load I'm stoned and
        bled?"

CIV

O, Rabby, shame us not, if we are all
The products of a monstrous Sin, a Fall;
    How then will Milk and Honey ever flow,
If the eternal Source is bitter Gall?

CV

Why contemplate, why analyze and test,
If Man then is the same from East to West?
His word is perfidy, his love a lie,
His good is evil and his health a pest.

CVI

His smile, a makeshift; what he knows, a curse;
His riches, blighting poverty and worse;
    His wisdom, folly, and his faith a sham—
Why ponder, why dissect, in prose or verse?

CVII

If miracles were wrought in bygone years,
Why not to-day, why not to-day, O, seers?
    This Leprous Age, aye, needs a healing
        hand,
Why heed not then his cries and dry his tears?

CVIII

Fan thou the fire and then behold the light!
Fan thou but ashes and bemoan thy sight:
    Call thou the living and they will respond,
But whom thou callest are as dead as Night.

CIX

The path of Wrong is broader than the sky,
The path of Right is like the needle's eye;
 The Soul, unless she's whipp'd, will travel
  not
Through it, her "Wherefor?" ceasing, "Whence
  and Why?"

CX

"How oft, O Soul?" I said in my despair,

"This Garment is too good for thee to wear,"

    And thou wouldst answer: "I had not my

        choice,

So free me from these chains of Whence and

        Where."

CXI

Whence come, O, firmament, those myriad
      lights,
Whence comes thy juice, O, vine on yonder
      heights?
Whence comes the perfume of the rose, and
      whence
The Soul that with this flesh forever fights?

CXII

Whence does the nettle get its bitter sting?
Whence do the honey-bees their honey bring?
    A thousand questions thou wilt ask in vain,
I know not, I repeat, one single thing.

CXIII

How many, like us, in the ages past
Have blindly soared, tho' like a pebble cast,
    Seeking the veil of Mystery to tear,
But fell accursed 'neath the burning blast?

CXIV

"A hell," some shriek; its fire tho' I do know
Is set by evil Deeds, that in it blow;
    Our hells we make and unmake as we live—
The flames that smoke and burn will warm and
      glow.

CXV

How like a Door the knowledge we would gain,
Which Door is on the bourne of the Inane;
    It opens and our Nothingness is closed;
It closes and in Darkness we remain.

CXVI

Why delve then in the sod, or search the sky

For Truths, alas! which neither you nor I

    Can grasp, since Death alone the Secret

        keeps

And will impart it to us by and by?

CXVII

How many Sultans 'cended from a throne,
To journey through the dust, to that Unknown?
    They went forth naked and behind them
        left
A kingdom desolate, in panic thrown.

CXVIII

But even Sultans will to Clay return
And, chancing, serve us as a coffee urn;
    Perchance remoulded to a pot and then
Drinks from it whoso wishes in his turn:

CXIX

It may be carried from its native land,
Where on its throne it once did wield the wand;
   Alas! the Sultan never thought that he
Would dwell with tipplers on the beach's sand.

CXX

Is it ordained that this Adamic race
Be even in Death in Sorrow's strong embrace?
    Felicitate the kindred of the dead—
Theirs is the legacy and his the grace.

CXXI

Thou art the creature of thy Present Age,
Thy Past is an obliterated Page;
    The rest that follows may not see thee more,
Make best of what is worst and do not rage.

CXXII

Aye, kiss the dimpled cheeks of New-born Day
And hail Eternity in every ray,
    That forms a halo round its infant head,
And lights up with its fiery Eye the way.

CXXIII

Enchained in blindness of both Faith and Sight,
I two long nights make of my darkest Night;
    Once Ummu-lila luring I espoused,
But even she my darkness could not light.

CXXIV

This eye, as Life endures, the heir will be
To sleeplessness, this Soul, to jealousy;
  This body, heir to illness, but this heart,
Heir to that hope that may yet set us free.

CXXV

And now these Daughters of my heart and mind,
I shield and keep secluded from mankind;
    They seek no son of man to win his heart,
Nor will they even wed a world unkind.

CXXVI

Farewell, my day! Thy like will never dawn
Upon this sightless face, once thou art gone—
   I'm always falling and will only rise
When I descend into the grave forlorn.

INTAHA.

NOTES

I

"Lîle" and "Lîlat," two words for night, are respectively masculine and feminine nouns. The first is used in a general sense, and the second, which is used with a definite article, is commonly accepted as a specific term.

II

This was doubtless written in his latter days when he was completely blind. It is invariably the custom among Arabic poets to preface their poems, regardless of the subject-matter, with a few amatory lines. Abu'l-Ala, having had no occasion to evince such tender emotions, succeeded, as in everything else he did, in deviating from the trodden path. I find, however, in his minor Diwan, called "Sact-uz-Zind," a slight manifestation of his youthful days, which, of course, is the only exception to the foregoing statement. These are the few quatrains with which I choose to open this eclogue.

IV

In the first quatrain the poet speaks of night in a general sense, and therefore uses the masculine noun. He here compares his one Night to an Ethiop queen, using the feminine noun instead. When I first read these lines in the original, I thought the figure was rather grotesque, and hesitated about introducing it into the poem. I see, however, that Milton, in his "Il Penseroso," speaks of the "starred Ethiop queen," and Romeo, speaking of Juliet, says: "Her beauty hangs upon the cheek of night as a rich jewel in an Ethiop ear." The simile of Shakespeare and the metaphor of Abu'l-Ala are not exactly alike, but the same ruling thought is nevertheless conspicuous in both.

VIII

The same thought is expressed less strikingly by Omar Khayyam. Here are the first three

lines of the 122nd quatrain of the Heron-Allen's
literal translation:

> "To him who understands the mysteries of the
> world,
> The joy and sorrow of the world is all the
> same,
> Since the good and the bad of the world all
> come to an end."

X

"Aad," the name of a tribe that flourished
in Arabia in ancient Pagan times, many centuries before Christ.

XII

I quote again from Omar's for the purpose
of showing the similarity of thought that exists
between the two poets. Following is the
twentieth quatrain of Fitzgerald's version,
fourth edition:

> "And this reviving Herb, whose Tender Green
> Fledges the River-Lip, on which we lean—
> Ah, lean upon it lightly! for who knows
> From what once lovely Lip it springs unseen."

In justice to both poets, however, this quatrain and the literal translation of it should appear side by side. Here, then, is the forty-third quatrain of Heron-Allen's translation, which I think contains two lines of that of Fitzgerald:

"Everywhere that there has been a rose or
    tulip bed
There has been spilled the crimson blood of a
    king;
Every violet shoot that grows from the earth
Is a mole that was once upon the cheek of a
    beauty."

XX

It was Tennyson who wrote:

"There is more truth in honest doubt,
Believe me, than in all the creeds."

XXI

"Benat'ul-Hadeel," daughters of Hadeel, is a poetic term for doves. Hadeel is also the name of a particular dove that died of thirst in the days of Noah, and all the members of his family, as mythology has it, still weep for him till this day.

XXIII

He longs for certainty, he thirsts for knowledge, but he knows that the intellectual faculties of man can not reach the depth or the height of the beyond. There is the feverish desire to know, but not the means. There is the Pail, but not the Rope. How appropriate and powerful the figure! How cogent the argument! How true the idea!

XXIV

He here compares the Soul to the Bole of a tree, and the mind, conscience and will to the branches that spring from it. If, then, he hearken to the voice of his soul, and commit suicide, will he not annihilate the mind and conscience or conscientious self as well? Let the reader compare this and the succeeding quatrain with the famous soliloquy of Hamlet, and the similarity in the trend of thought will

---

be apparent. I do not, however, claim as much depth for the Arabic poet, who prefers drowning to the bare bodkin.

XXV

I quote again from Omar, Fitzgerald's version quatrain 44:

"Why, if the Soul can fling the Dust aside,
And naked on the air of Heaven ride,
    Were't not a shame—were't not a shame
        for him
In this clay carcass, crippled to abide?"

And from Heron-Allen's quatrain 145:

"O Soul, if thou canst purify thyself from the
    dust of the clay,
Thou, naked spirit, canst soar in the heav'ns,
The Empyrian is thy sphere—let it be thy shame
That thou comest and art a dweller within the
    confines of earth."

Throughout the poem I use the feminine pronoun for "An-Nafs," soul, my reason being

that the Arabic noun is of the feminine gender
and rightly so, since femininity is more becom-
ing of the soul.

XXVI

The human soul and the human conscience
are not to him convertible terms, although this
idea of oneness was expounded by many of the
scholars of his time.

XXXIII

This led some of his enemies to accuse him
of pure materialism, which accusation, however,
can easily be repelled by the citation of many
other poems, taken at random from his Diwan.

XXXIV

Omar was also a confessed cynical-hypocrite.
Thus runs the first line of the 114th quatrain
of Heron-Allen's.

"The world being fleeting, I practise naught
but artifice."

And he also chafes in the chains of his sins. Following is the twenty-third quatrain of the same translation:

"Khayyam, why mourn for thy sins?
From grieving thus what advantage more or
    less dost thou gain?
Mercy was never for him who sins not,
Mercy is granted for sins: why then grieve?"

I remember that Abu'l-Ala asks in one of his poems which I have not translated, "Why do good, since you are to be forgiven for thy sins?"

XL

"Käba Stone," the black stone in the Käba at Mecca, which the Mohammedans regard as sacred.

LIII

He refers here to the Millenium which the Christians in the latter part of the tenth century anticipated. Students of history will observe how the delusion fastened itself on the

mind of Christian Europe, and how, in conse-
quence of the same, every branch of industry,
commerce and art was brought to a standstill.
Arabia, it seems, was infected by the disease,
and Abu'l-Ala could not but prescribe a remedy.

LVIII

The state of things has almost remained the
same from the time of Abu'l-Ala down to the
days when the American poet exclaimed:
"Truth forever on the scaffold, wrong forever
on the throne."

LXIII

He refers to the quarrels and contentions of
the Jews, the Mohammedans and the Christians,
concerning the Sabbath day, Friday being that
of the Mohammedans.

LXIV

"Rabbik," thy God.

137

LXVIII

This is the quatrain a paraphrastic translation of which appears in Carlisle's Specimen of Arabic Poetry.

LXXV

How often does Omar repeat the idea of Cash and Credit in the Heron-Allen version. It seems to me that this is a sister idea to the "drink and make merry" one. Abu'l-Ala, however, though a plain and unornamented pessimist, has harped on this same string before him. The idea of Cash and Credit, clothed in various garbs and representing divers conditions and situations, is profusely scattered throughout the Diwan.

LXXVI

Many other Arabic poets lament the frequency of calamities, the fickleness of fortune and the obduracy of Fate and recommend resignation, fortitude, courage and temperance as assuaging remedies.

LXXVII

Galen, the famous Greek physician who lived in the second century.

Bocrates, the Arabic for Hippocrates, the "Father of Medicine," who lived in the fifth century, B. C.

LXXXI

Shakespeare, in "Measure for Measure," evinces like sympathy by expressing a similar idea. Isabella, speaking to her brother, says:

"And the poor beatle, that we tread upon,
In corporal sufferance finds a pang as great
As when a giant dies."

LXXXV

He likens Youth to the Raven, whose feathers are black, and Age to the Falcon, with his rich white plumage. The idea of the darkness of folly in Youth and the light of wisdom in Age is beautifully and delicately suggested. Baha-ud-Deen-Zoheir, whose poems are translated into English by E. H. Palmer, expresses this same idea with more vividness and lucidity. I cannot resist the temptation of quoting it here:

"Now the night of youth is over and the gray
    head dawn is near,
Fare ye well ye tender meetings, with the friends
    I held so dear;
O'er my life these silvery locks are shedding an
    unwonted light,
And disclosing many follies youth has hidden
    out of sight."

Of course Zoheir expands and Abu'l-Ala only suggests.

XCVIII

"Khodour," a plural noun signifying boudoirs: the apartment of the harem.

This and the two succeeding quatrains I have chosen from numerous poems he composed on this topic. His antipathy for marriage was not less vehement than his hatred for all that was false in the teachings of monks, sheiks and rabbis. This is a literal translation of the epitaph he wrote for himself:

"My father thus did wrong me,
And I have no one wronged."

XCIX

Omar and Khalid, two popular masculine names in Arabia corresponding to the American Jones and Smith. The next quatrain elucidates the meaning of this one.

CII

The pronoun here reverts to man. Contemporary students and ardent admirers of Abu'l-Ala have made much of the thought expressed in this quatrain. "Man," says the poet, "is evolved from inorganic matter." (I use the specific term clay for the sake of the rhyme only.) And so, in two lines, they say, this poet has expounded, in the early centuries, the theory of evolution, which was perfected by Lamark and Darwin. They forget that the fancy of the poet may sometimes be in harmony with the logical conclusions of the scientists; but this does not warrant us in classifying the former with the latter.

CIV

"Rabby," my God.

CVII

He refers to the leper who was healed by Christ, but not without an insinuation of doubt mingled with sarcasm.

CX

Here is Omar Khayyam's idea of this matter, taken from Heron-Allen's 157th quatrain:

"Had I charge of the matter I would not have
　　come,
And likewise could I control my going, where
　　could I go?"

Abu'l-Ala says elsewhere that had he come

142

here of his own accord he would be biting his ten fingers in repentance. This idea he often repeats in his poems, and I have only chosen what appears here as a fair specimen.

CXIV

The same idea is expressed by Omar. I quote from quatrain sixty-six of Fitzgerald's version:

"And by and by my Soul came back to me
And answered I myself am Heav'n and Hell."

CXVIII–CXIX

This reminds me of Hamlet's words on Cæsar:

"Imperial Cæsar, dead and turned to clay,
Might stop a hole to keep the wind away;
O, that that earth, which kept the world in awe,
Should stop a wall t'expell the winter's flaw!"

CXXI

I must again have recourse to Omar for comparison. Following is Heron-Allen's twelfth quatrain:

"Thou hast no power over the morrow,
And anxiety about the morrow is useless to thee;
    Waste not thou the moment, if thy heart
        is not mad,
For the value of the remainder of thy life is not
        manifest."

CXXIII

He refers to his blindness and his skepticism. "Ummu-līla," an Arabic term for black wine. In all his poems, published in three volumes, this is the only reference I find to his ever indulging in wine. He was abstemious in habit, and in numerous poems scattered in desultory fashion throughout the three volumes he denounces with the enthusiasm of a modern prohibitionist, "the old familiar juice."

CPSIA information can be obtained at www.ICGtesting.com
Printed in the USA
LVOW11s2029011013

354950LV00015B/379/P